# Shattered

*Through the Heartbreak and Healing of Abortion*
*A 31-Day Devotional Journey*

by M.L Alvarez

There was a time when I was innocent, the day before my life shattered into a myriad of pieces. Unequal shards, each casting a glimmer of light, but inwardly holding onto the darkness.

Not seeing an end to the pain, the loss. No end to the emptiness.

I was enveloped by darkness, not seeing my potential to cascade the light off of my serrated pieces that still lay where they were scattered. Unable to see that I still held beauty inside me.

If I opened my eyes to the truth, to the possibilities, things might have been different, but then I might have been a different me.

I like the me I am.

- mla

This book is dedicated to you dear reader.

May God grant you the courage to open up your heart, let his grace inside and envelope you.  May you see clearly His love for you.

# Table of Contents

# Intro

*Genesis 50:20: You intended to harm me, but God intended it for good to accomplish what is now being done, the saving of many lives (NIV).*

It was ten years after my abortion when I realized I needed healing. I was lost in the darkness of my abortion. Perhaps you, like me, went through some sort of post-abortive healing group after your own experience. Or maybe you have held on to your secret since the day you had your abortion. I pray this book meets you where you are and allows God to comfort and heal the places you might not be ready to reveal to others. Just know that you can open those hurts to him and allow his light to begin restoring the dark places.

Even if you did go through a healing group, feelings of shame can start to creep back into your mind. You start to believe what the devil is speaking to you. You may easily lose sight of the truth that God has healed you and made you a new creation. As 1 Corinthians 6:11 says, the person you were before is gone. Now you are washed, sanctified, and justified in the name of the Lord Jesus Christ and in the Spirit of our God.

God can take away those shameful feelings and he can battle for you. I know, because he has done this for me. I am amazed how God can take the one thing in my life that was a gaping, infected wound and use it for his glory. I have witnessed many women lightened of the burden of abortion. I am confident that if God can do that with me and other women, he will do it for you too.

By using my story in this way, God continues to heal me, helping me make peace with my past. Through my healing journey, I've learned more about myself, and more about God. The scar and some of the pain is still there, but I no longer feel the desperation, depression, shame, or hopelessness that once haunted me.

One gal likened the post-abortive journey to an onion. We peel back each of the layers and reveal just enough pain to deal with each day, each week. It's good to remember that we don't have to regurgitate all of our past at once. God is okay with revealing what we can handle day by day.

I don't know where you are at on your journey. But wherever that is, may God meet you where you are.

# How to Use This Devotional

When I began to write this devotional, I had no agenda. God simply placed the thought into my heart to write a devotional about abortion, and I wondered why I hadn't thought of it sooner. But God's timing is better than mine, so I trust in that.

I desire for you use to use this devotional where you are at, right now. Please do not be overwhelmed by the questions or journaling spaces. They are there for women, like me, who might want to jot down some thoughts as they read. You can read the questions and see if they spark anything in you, or you can skip them altogether.

I wrote these devotional thoughts with many of you in mind. I reflected about myself right after my abortion, in the years following, and even the years since I began my healing journey, hoping you would find connection and encouragement from my experience. Through the initial writing and each draft, I have been praying for you. I pray that you might pick up this devotional and find the same healing in the same God as I did. The God that created you and formed you. I pray that if you feel the doubt and shame coming up again you will remember the words God has spoken to you on your journey. You are beautiful. You are loved. You are forgiven. You are free from your past. And you are healed.

May God direct your path.

*Faith is a living, daring confidence in God's grace, so sure and certain that a man could stake his life on it a thousand times. -Martin Luther*

# Day One: Broken

*Psalm 147:3: He heals the brokenhearted and binds up their wounds (NASB).*

Whenever I'm in the doctor's office and I have to put my feet in the cold stirrups, I am immediately taken back to that day in the abortion clinic. I can feel the cold stainless steel table beneath the thin paper covering and hear the muted cries from women around me. When I look back to that day, I wonder how I survived.

It was 1993. The drive to the clinic took about thirty minutes. Not many words passed between us in the car, and I secretly hoped there would be a crowd of protestors, that my boyfriend would give in and tell me I didn't have to go through with it. Above all I wanted him to rescue me and tell me that we could figure things out.

But that didn't happen.

Instead, like a cow being led to slaughter, the clinic staff brought me to the back rooms. Over the next six hours, I was herded to different stations to fill out paperwork, have blood drawn, receive an ultrasound, and change into my "comfy clothes," as if they would make it all better. I was given a pill to relax me and one to begin the contractions. I looked at the tiny paper cup with the blue and white pills, and remember thinking, *I don't have to take them.* I could toss them and go home. But what would be waiting for me on the outside?

Nothing. If I didn't do this, my boyfriend would leave me. It sounds silly now, but at the time I was alone in a different state, far away from anyone who cared about me.

When the procedure was done, we were brought into a room filled with cots. If I hadn't known better, I would have thought I was back at Girl Scout camp. I received a cookie and some juice. And when I was able to hold that down, we were free to go.

I walked down the hallway and out the front door, leaving the clinic behind me. There was a rush of emotions that bubbled to the surface, like an unwanted visitor. A part of me felt relief, followed by guilt, and the rest were feelings I couldn't quite explain.

Things were different now. *I* was different, though I didn't fully understand that back then.

That was the day my life shattered and separated like pieces of a puzzle.

**Reflection Questions:**

• Can you remember the day that things changed for you? It might not have been your abortion(s), but choices you made before that. What were the moments that forever changed you?

• Take time to think about your abortion(s). Use a journal to write down the events you remember from that day. How do you think your abortion has affected your life since it occurred?

_____

_____

_____

_____

_____

**Prayer:**

*Lord, help me to dig deep into the sensitive places of my heart and remember that day. The day that my choice broke something within me. Please fill up the empty places with grace and love. Lord, my desire is to be whole. I want to come out on the other side of this feeling restored to all you created me to be. May it be like your word says, may I become like the "oaks of righteousness, a planting of the LORD for the display of his splendor" (Isaiah 61:3 NIV).*

# Day Two: The Vow

*1 John 1:9: If we confess our sins, he is faithful and just to forgive us our sins and to cleanse us from all unrighteousness (ESV).*

After my abortion I walked out of the clinic, down the steps toward the car. I was overcome by torrents of emotion, cascading over me like floodwaters. I felt stuck in their rushing rapids, unable to breathe. I remember experiencing relief as it poured out of me. But I also remember the anger and hatred that filled me back up.

And I remember the vow. The vow that I would never have more children.

I didn't realize it at the time, but looking back, that was the moment when my heart began to harden. I took the anger, the feelings of betrayal from being forced into this situation, and I held on to it all. Soon it took root and developed a life all its own. I told myself that I couldn't be trusted with another child after what I had done with the one I was given. I didn't deserve another chance. These thoughts became a constant cadence in my head, and most of my decisions after the abortion surrounded that one vow.

I never became pregnant again.

Our life is a series of choices. Each one influencing the next. I made many reckless decisions, but it could have been worse. Even though I didn't believe in God at the time, he believed in me. He kept me from becoming completely lost to everyone.

It's important to know that wherever we have been, whatever we have done, God loves us and will be there with open arms to welcome us back home. We can choose to ignore our feelings and allow our wounds to fester, or we can seek God and allow his healing power into our hearts. He alone healed me and brought me to life. He wants to do the same for you.

**Reflection Questions:**

- If you, like me, made a vow with yourself—either consciously or unconsciously—what was it?

- Read and meditate on Genesis 50:20; If you want, read the full account of Joseph in Genesis 37-50.

- Do you believe you are worth healing? God wants to remove your hurt and make you whole. Write down any destructive choices you made after your abortion. Bring them into the light, and ask God to restore those places in your heart.

_____

_____

_____

_____

_____

**Prayer:**

*Lord, please hear my confession and cleanse me. Show the places within me that need your healing touch and power. Give me the strength to renounce any destructive vows that came from that day or anytime after. Help me to move forward in freedom from anything that has left me chained to the past. Help me to move forward in victory.*

# Day Three: Truth

*John 8:32: . . . and you will know the truth, and the truth will make you free (NASB).*

I recently heard this lyric in a song: "We hold the light, but we still listen to the dark." So many times I get caught up in the darkness. I think about what I did, and I allow it to speak to me. It tells me how terrible I am, that I am a failure, that there is no hope. In the thick, black night, my soul festers and rots.

In order for God to come in and redeem those dark parts of us, we need to know the stark truth. We might not want this, we might fight it all the way. But once we lay it out, there is nothing left to fear. There are no more secrets about what we thought happened, or the lies we were told. We are faced with reality; that it was a child. And it's not until we face this truth that we can begin to grieve our loss.

When I had my abortion, my child was nine weeks along.

- At 19 days a baby's heart begins to beat.
- At 35 days the eyes start to develop and 40 pairs of muscles are present.
- At 42 days brain waves are detectable.
- At 49 days the skeletal system is developed. The baby appears as a miniature doll with complete fingers, toes, and ears.
- At 56 days all organs are functioning.
- At the ninth and tenth week teeth begin to form, fingernails develop, and the baby can squint and swallow.

I experienced morning sickness that I hid from my daycare coworkers. The truth stared at me everyday, but I ignored it. I chose to believe it was a clump of cells, like many people had told me, because it was easier. Learning the details about my baby was difficult, but it was necessary for God to work in my heart. Once it sunk in that the "clump of cells" I had carried was actually a child, my sins were thrust into the light, and that's when I finally began to taste the promised freedom. Because I had nothing left to hide.

God had seen me for what I truly was, and he wanted me still. And then he went a step further, and he offered to forgive and redeem me. He's offering the same to you.

**Reflection Questions:**

- At the abortion clinic what were you told about your child?

- What do you believe is the truth about your child?

- What were some ways you tried to hide the truth from others or from yourself?

_____

_____

_____

_____

_____


**Prayer:**

*Lord, let your healing reign in me. Open up the places of darkness that I think I can keep to myself. Shine your light on those places and heal as only you have the power to do. Lord, I have tried to hide so many of these places, but you want me to bow at your knees and confess. I no longer need to cover up my mistakes and try and place a bow on such a muddy package. It seems ridiculous, but I do it all the time. Grant me the courage to come clean about all the things in my past and by your light and counsel, I will remain clean.*

# Day Four: Happy Mother's Day

*Isaiah 49:15: "Can a mother forget the baby at her breast and have no compassion on the child she has borne? Though she may forget, I will not forget you!" (NIV).*

For me, Mother's Day is anything but happy. This day comes with a lot of heaviness, not only for my abortion but for the many losses this day represents. It's like a special day for me to remember all the regret, hurt, failure, and betrayal.

When I was around ten years old, my parents came home one day and something was different. Being curious, I made mention of it, and my words sent my mother crying to her room. As I was making a Mother's Day card for her the next day, my father told me that it wasn't enough to make up for the hurt I had caused the night before.

That memory is just one of many that led me to dislike a day set aside for mothers. This day is a constant reminder, a finger tapping on my heart to the rhythm "you will never be a mother." It makes me think of what will never be and what I did when I became a mother for a brief moment in time.

How do I turn it around? How do I quench the desire to run away and hide when this day hits? I have not figured it out yet, and I know I'm not the only one. But I also know that women who are mothers, like my sister and many of my friends, deserve a day to be celebrated for getting it right. They may not be perfect, but they are sticking it out in the trenches every day and doing the best they can. And if I can use

Mother's Day to offer them a kind and encouraging word, instead of sinking in my own past regrets, I might just find a way to survive this difficult holiday.

**Reflection Questions:**

- Is Mother's Day hard for you? Maybe you have other children, so it's bittersweet. Or maybe you and your own mother don't get along. What kind of feelings does this holiday stir up in you?

- If you, like me, are not a mother, are there people in your life who could use your guidance and care? Make a list of people you believe you could impart your wisdom and love on during the year.

- Is there a mother you could encourage on Mother's Day with a card, note, or phone call?

_____

_____

_____

_____

_____

**Prayer:**

*Lord, I cling to this verse, that you will never forget me and we will never forget our child! I pray that when I start to have these negative feelings about Mother's Day, you will remind me that I am not forgotten. My child is not forgotten. Help me to see this day not as a reminder of how I failed, but as a way to celebrate those that gave life. Quiet the voice in my head that tells me all the reasons I am not worthy of being a mother. Show me any way I can be a mother to those around me. I acknowledge that this is a struggle, but you have been faithful in the past, and I trust you will be in this as well.*

# Day Five: Not Alone

*Isaiah 41:10: Fear not, for I am with you; be not dismayed, for I am your God; I will strengthen you, I will help you, I will uphold you with my righteous right hand (ESV).*

Before the abortion, it was easy to buy into the lies. This would solve our problems and we could move on from here, live our life. It would be like it never happened.

Unfortunately, that's not how it works out. The reality is, we will remember. We will think about it again and again. Sure, we felt a little relief at first. But the secret we have tried to hide will keep bubbling back up, a reverberating echo in our souls.

We remember when we are at baby showers. When our nieces and nephews are born. When our friends have children. We begin to wonder what if? What could have been? We hear the word abortion in church or in conversation and the shame ignites in us. We wonder when we will be found out. Some of us have experienced trouble getting pregnant and wondered if that is our punishment. Some of us have felt guilty about having more children after our abortion, knowing in our hearts that there were one, two, or three more children that we could have held.

Most of us will never forget about our abortion. We cannot stop the memories from surfacing. But we *can* change the way we think about it.

There is hope. You are not alone. Statistics show that 43 percent of all women will have at least one abortion by the time they are 45 years old. There are many of us hurting from our abortions out there. I am one of them. I have met many more. And God cares deeply about us all.

God continues to pursue you and call you back to him. He loves you with an everlasting love that cannot be measured, and he has collected all of your tears in a bottle. (Psalm 56:8) You are important to him. He would lay down his life for *just you*. God can heal your heart and take this abortion and use it for his glory. It might sound too good to be true. But he did this for me, and that's why I know he will also do it for you.

**Reflection Questions:**

- How does it make you feel knowing that God has collected all of your tears in a bottle?

- Is there someone that you trust, that you could share your abortion story with? Maybe you just write it out for yourself.

- God loves you and pursues you always. How does that truth make you feel?

- In what ways have you seen his pursuit for you?

_____

_____

_____

_____

_____

**Prayer:**

*Father God, please strengthen me as you have promised. Let me remember clearly the ways you have pursued me. I am in awe that you have remembered all my tears and collected them in a bottle just for me. I am not alone, you are with me. Lift the heavy burden off of me. Amaze me with your healing power. Give me the freedom you have promised. Teach me to take up your yoke and learn from you. Give me rest. And as you bless me, may I become a blessing to others, encouraging them to see that they are not alone.*

# Day Six: Left Behind

*Luke 15:4: "What man among you, if he has a hundred sheep and has lost one of them, does not leave the ninety-nine in the open pasture and go after the one which is lost until he finds it?" (NASB).*

There is a parable in the bible about a shepherd who has one hundred sheep and will leave the ninety-nine to find the one that was lost. I think our abortion experiences are similar. We can fill our lives up with children and possessions and things to do, but we will never forget the one we left behind. If you hide that memory and let it fester, it will only become infected. The precious child will remain a dark secret, a stain on your heart. But when you bring your experience into the light, it is remarkable what God will do.

When you share your secret for the first time, you make it real. You give flesh to it. It becomes a reality and a child. Though the harshness of what you did remains, there are positive things you can do now. You can receive forgiveness. You can begin to heal. And you have permission to grieve.

But that shepherd parable doesn't just apply to the children we lost. I can also see myself as the lost sheep and how God never gave up on me. He never left me behind, and he won't leave you behind either. It is comforting to know that our God is a God of miracles—in people, in circumstances. Even though we are unworthy, God searches the ends of the earth, longing to bring us back home. His love astounds me.

**Reflection Questions:**

- How do you see yourself—are you part of the ninety-nine sheep in the fold, or are you the one sheep that was lost?

- How does it make you feel to know that God will not leave you behind, that he will pursue you?

_____

_____

_____

_____

_____


**Prayer:**

*Father, sometimes it feels like a cruel joke that I cannot forget about what I have done. I try to fill up my life with experiences, things, and people. I try to stay busy, because if I stop, I might feel the things I am so desperately running away from. I might stop long enough to see the truth. Fill me up with you Lord. Your word says that you will leave the flock to get the one sheep that ran astray. Help me to remember this truth that you care so deeply for me, that I am that one sheep. May I feel your love daily, and may I remember that you will never give up pursuit of me.*

# Day Seven: While We Were Still Sinners?

*Romans 5:8: But God demonstrates His own love toward us, in that while we were yet sinners, Christ died for us (NASB).*

After so many years of learning about God, it's starting to sink in how much God really loves me. In our humanness it is hard to imagine a God that loves so unconditionally. He died for each and every one of us, not while we were perfect and making all the right choices, but while we were killing, robbing, stealing, and lying. He knew the world was imperfect and there was no way we would make the cut. So he sent his Son to be that sacrificial lamb for you and I.

The cross shows us the immeasurable love of God. While we were still sinners Christ died for us. It really is that simple. God knew the choice I was going to make, and he loved me anyway. He died for me so that I wouldn't have to bear the punishment for what I had done. He who knew no sin, bore my sin for me. I can't say I would do that for someone I know and love, let alone someone who was a stranger to me.

It is hard to imagine a love that goes so deep because we don't live this way. We don't give our love away; it has strings and conditions. But God freely gives of himself. No matter where we are at in our lives, he loves. No matter what we have done, he forgives. It doesn't matter how far off the mark we've fallen, he redeems. He is the potter, and we are the broken clay he gently restores.

### Reflection Questions:

- Do you believe God loves you like his Word says he does? Why or why not?

- What do you feel is required of you for God to love, forgive, redeem, and restore you?

- When I say it is as simple as accepting the forgiveness God freely gives, what arguments come up in your heart and mind?

- God loves you just as you are. What would it look like to come to him right now, not when you think you have it all together?

**Optional Exercise:** Write a letter to someone explaining God's forgiveness and love. Then read it as if it was written to you.

_____

_____

_____

_____

_____

### Prayer:

*Lord, your immeasurable love can only come from your hand. Let me feel that love deep in the empty recesses of my heart. Please let your forgiveness wash over me and fill up those empty spaces. Expand my faith to believe your grace cancel out even this wrong. Help me to move forward as a confident child of God. May I shed any feelings of unworthiness and hold my head high. May I remember that I am the daughter of a risen King!*

# Day Eight: Thunder & Lightning

*Ephesians 4:26-27: Be angry and yet do not sin, . . . and do not give the devil an opportunity (NASB).*

Anger has always been one of those friends that is both good and bad for me. Every time we are together, we pick up where we left off, and it escalates from there. Afterward, I am usually sickened by my actions, but right in the middle of my outbursts, there is this exhilaration that flourishes from the release of all this restrained rage. For a long time, I couldn't stop this cycle.

Until I broke my hand.

It was during high school when I first started punching lockers. And since then, I may have punched a hole (or two) in an apartment wall. Most of these incidents were simply me being young and dumb. My anger was explosive, and it would shoot out, uncontrolled. But the night I punched a small wall built out of solid studs, I was nearing forty and I knew better. I felt the bubbling rage and allowed it to fuel the flame. And it was my choice to let my anger out in a violent manner. With my unfortunate luck, the wall I punched didn't budge and I knew right away, my hand was broken.

Sure enough, I shattered my pinky knuckle. Thankfully the doctor thought it would heal without surgery. And it did. My stupid act didn't cost too much monetarily, but the message did finally sink in. It's important to express anger in healthy ways.

As I worked toward healthier ways of handling my feelings, I knew that part of my anger came from my past abortion. And it was okay to be angry with those involved with my abortion decision. It was okay to be angry with people that robbed me of my innocence. It was even okay to be angry with myself. When we see victims of injustice—whether ourselves or others—it *should* anger us. The problem with anger is that it doesn't serve us well when we dwell on it. If anger is all there is, it will just lead to bitterness and destruction. We have to release that anger, channeling it into something we are passionate about and using it to fuel a change for causes greater than ourselves.

I still feel mad at times. But now when I feel the spark of anger, I remember that it doesn't have to turn into a violent fire. I can still be angry. But when I steer that anger toward my passion for reaching post-abortive women, the uncontrollable rage fizzles. And instead, it becomes the fuel that helps me share God's healing love.

**Reflection Questions:**

- When you think about your abortion(s), what does it spark within you?

- What are some ways you have expressed your anger in the past?

- What are some healthier ways you can express your anger?

_____

_____

_____

_____

_____

**Prayer:**

*Lord, help me to seek healthy ways to release my anger. Help me to not give the devil a foothold by giving him access to my anger. If I am in denial about being angry, help me to see the truth about myself no matter what it reveals. I might only be angry with myself for the choice I ultimately made. No matter what it is, I know that the truth will set me free and that is how I will move forward to be fully healed from this. Help me to channel my anger—toward the purposes and passions you have written on my heart.*

# Day Nine: Let Go

*1 Peter 5:7: Casting all your anxieties on him, because he cares for you (ESV).*

When I attended my first abortion healing group, I remember sitting in class and telling my story as if I were a bystander. I didn't realize how disconnected I was from my story. I felt the emotion bubbling up, but I pinched my arm, clenched my jaw, and tightened my fists. Anything to keep the feelings inside. I refused to give in to the overflow of emotion surging from the deep valley within me, a place that hadn't seen the light since my child was torn from me.

I regret holding it all in that day. The leader of the group encouraged me to let it out, but I wasn't comfortable. This was only our second meeting and I didn't know these people. I also wanted to be strong, to keep up the facade that it didn't hurt, that I was fine. But the pressure was too great; a few tears spilled out, but nothing like the flood that wanted to pour out of me. The tension had to go somewhere, and it physically manifested itself in a massive migraine.

To this day, I struggle with emotions. I fight them. I don't want to seem needy, put my guard down, or appear weak. But I am learning to let go and be free, remembering that it's in our weakness where God shows his strength.

Even though I knew God had forgiven me, it took many years for me to fully understand God's love and forgiveness. Before I could allow the healing to sink in, I needed to come to terms with my abortion. I needed to let out my pain and shame before it consumed me. I pray you can open up to someone safe, someone you trust. Release your emotions before they eat you alive. Remember, God's strength shines brightest in our weakness. With him, it will always be safe to let those pent-up feelings go.

**Reflection Questions:**

- What feelings or memories surrounding your abortion(s) have you been holding in?

- What fears keep you from letting them go?

- List one thing you could do today that would be a small step toward a healing journey.

_____

_____

_____

_____

_____

**Prayer:**

*Lord, I pray for the peace of release. Help me to liberate my emotions safely in your presence. I am very tired trying to plug all the leaks that spring forth. Help me to cast my cares and fears at your feet. Help me to see there is safety and healing inside your wings. In my weakness is where your glory burns bright and by your strength alone we are able to live free.*

# Day Ten: Forgiveness

*Ephesians 4:32: Be kind to one another, tender-hearted, forgiving each other, just as God in Christ also has forgiven you (NASB).*

I love this saying: "Unforgiveness is like drinking poison and hoping your enemy dies." It's true; I can hold a grudge, thinking I am punishing the person who betrayed me, but in the end it only hurts me and keeps me in bondage.

When it came to my abortion, the person I thought I could never forgive was myself. I thought I was doing the best thing by punishing myself for failing my child. And I didn't just punish myself for the abortion, I did this anytime I failed. I thought this strategy would rid me of the wound I created, but it only drove the knife in deeper and twisted it.

These same feelings drove me to vow to myself that I'd never have children. I decided I didn't deserve to have children. More punishment.

Years later, I finally understood. I didn't need to forgive myself; I needed to accept God's forgiveness, already there for me. This forgiveness was a gift God handed to me when he sent his son to die on a cross so that I could live a life of freedom. By refusing to forgive myself for my abortion, I was saying that Christ's sacrifice wasn't good enough. That he should die an additional death for my abortion. But who was I to think that? It's not my job to decide what sins God died for—he's already decided, and he's told us clearly that he died for them all.

As I learned to embrace God's forgiveness, I also needed to take an account of who I was angry with, who I blamed for my abortion. The bulk of my anger was focused on myself, but it was healing to acknowledge who else had a hand in the abortion and let them have their part of the blame.

When it comes to forgiving other people who played a part in your abortion decision, it's good to remember that you don't have to reconcile or even talk to them. You don't have to forget about what happened to you or how it affected your life. Releasing them from the hold they have on you is a process. Sometimes you will need to repeatedly forgive that person. It might start out as an hourly decision, then move to daily, weekly. Eventually you will only think about it when the emotion flares up from time to time.

Forgiving others—and yourself—can be a very long process. But through the process, you are setting yourself free.

**Reflection Questions:**

- Who do you need to forgive and set free in regards to your abortion?

- Do you find it hard to forgive yourself? Read John 8:1-11 and allow God's forgiveness to wash over you. He has not condemned you. How do you imagine God feels when you condemn yourself?

- Think beyond your abortion experience. Is there anyone else that you need to work on forgiving?

_____

_____

_____

_____

_____

**Prayer:**

*Lord, it is true that the hardest person to forgive is sometimes myself. I have been fooled into believing that I can carry out the best punishment for my sin. But it is not my job to impart judgment on myself or anyone else. Instead, you simply ask us to accept your forgiveness. Please help me to unwrap this generous gift of forgiveness. Let me allow your love to burst forth and tear down these lies and truly live free of this yoke of slavery.*

# Day Eleven: East to West

*Psalm 103:12: As far as the east is from the west, So far has He removed our transgressions from us (NASB).*

I once read something in a book that amplifies the meaning of God's promise to remove our sins as far as the east is from the west. The author described God's words in these terms: "If you go north, you can only go north so far until you're finally going south. And you can only go south so far until your going north. But if you start traveling east, it keeps going east forever, and west just keeps going west[1]." *That* is how far my sins, shortcomings, regret, pain, guilt, and shame have been cast from me. My job is to continue living with that truth, not living in the desolate pit. To accept the gifts God has given me.

I can easily wallow back into the muck of my past. It's so tempting to drown in my own sorrows. But God always nudges me, and I am reminded of his forgiveness. His forgiveness is a deep valley as much as it is a high mountain peak. There is no end to his love, patience, forgiveness, and grace. He freely gives and longs for us to accept everything he offers.

In our culture it is hard to imagine such unconditional love. We put lots of conditions on our friendships and relationships. So we struggle to comprehend a holy, loving, and unconditional God. Thankfully, God's love isn't limited by our imagination. So when you're tempted to dig up past mistakes, remember that God has already removed them from you. You don't need to carry that sin any longer; God has already cast it farther than the ends of the earth.

**Reflection Questions:**

• What does it feel like to know that your sin has been cast so far from you?

• What would it mean for you to accept the forgiveness God has already given?

• How could you live from this moment on, laying down the bonds of abortion—or anything else that keeps holding you back?

_____

_____

_____

_____

_____

**Prayer:**

*Lord, please walk with me through this desert in my life. I pray that I would experience your love and grace firsthand. I am beginning to realize that forgiveness is not just for everyone else, but it is for me too. Help me to know deeply that you have removed my sin as far as the east is from the west; and though I might never forget what I have done, I will remember also that your death on the cross covers it all. There is nothing you would not do for one of your children or one of mine. Help me to accept this gift you freely offer and live in freedom.*

# Day Twelve: Our Alabaster Jar

*Matthew 26:7: A woman came to Him with an alabaster vial of very costly perfume, and she poured it on His head as He reclined at the table. But the disciples were indignant when they saw this, and said, "Why this waste?" (NASB).*

When the woman with the alabaster jar poured her perfume over Jesus' head, his disciples thought she was foolish. Surely she could have done something better with the expensive perfume than wasting it in this fashion. But Jesus set his disciples straight. In his eyes, he explained, "She has done a beautiful thing."

That woman holding the perfume clearly believed that any price was worth the cost of drawing close to Jesus. Thinking about her story reminds me of my own journey toward forgiveness. There was a point in my healing story when all I wanted was forgiveness, and I would give up everything to get it.

I finally came to a point where I was willing to expose myself in order to be freed from the prison I had built around myself. In my prison there was a window, just wide enough to see what was going on around me. Just enough of a view to wish, to want, to hope for a better life. Of course, the walls I built were imagined. But for a long season of life, I lived as if I were behind bars, unable to show my pain or live in the freedom of God's forgiveness.

It took God reaching for me, taking ahold of my arm and helping me out, before I could finally break out of those self-imposed walls. If it weren't for his help, I would still be in there. God is always right there in the pit, ready to pull us out; we only need to see it or have someone help us see. It's not until our eyes are opened up that we can move forward in freedom. Then, we can break our own alabaster jars, recognizing that any price is worth paying to hold onto God's saving hands.

**Reflection Questions:**

- What is it you want more than anything?

- What is in your alabaster jar? Is there anything you have been holding tightly, that you need to give up for God?

- Do you see God reaching out to you in some way?

_____

_____

_____

_____

_____

**Prayer:**

*Lord, help me to see your hand reaching out to me. Take my shame and fears away so I can reach up and grab on to you for dear life. May I be as bold as the woman in the story and pour out my offerings to you, not only because you will save and heal, but because you have a larger purpose in plan for me. You are the true healer, God the Father, and you will not forsake me. I only need to ask for your healing. I am grateful and expectant for what you will accomplish in my life.*

# Day Thirteen: The Big A

*John 8:7: Let any one of you who is without sin be the first to throw a stone at her (NIV).*

There was a time when I would say there was a giant "A" on my soul. A for abortion. I thought about it all the time. Whenever I would hear the word, I would shrink back and hope that no one could see it stamped on me. During this season of my life, I would have said that I deserved all the guilt, the pain, and the shame I felt. It was a fitting punishment for throwing away what God gave to me. A life for a life.

One of the hardest things I had to come to terms with regarding forgiveness was that I needed to forgive myself. I came to realize that it wasn't just a matter of needing to forgive myself; what I really needed was to accept *God's* forgiveness. By holding on to this unforgiveness, by "punishing" myself, I was telling God that his death on the cross wasn't enough for me.

When I finally accepted God's forgiveness, the new freedom I felt was strange. I wanted to crawl back into the darkness and live where I thought it was safe. But that inner darkness was never really safe. Familiar maybe. But also self-destructive. At some point, I needed to shed the security blanket.

Jesus didn't die so that I could continue to wallow in my failures. He died so that I could live unencumbered and liberated from them.

I no longer feel the weight of the big "A" on my soul. Abortion no longer defines me. I am a woman who made a mistake, made a choice to have an abortion. But I now choose to embrace the forgiveness that covers my sin. I can continue to move forward in freedom. I don't wear a bright red "A" anymore, because I'm covered by the blood of Jesus to right this wrong.

### Reflection Questions:

- What sin do you slide back into because it is familiar?

- What are you defined by?

- What would your life look like if you lived out of this freedom that Jesus provided with the blood he shed for us? (Read the story about the adulterous woman in John 8:1-11)

_____

_____

_____

_____

_____

### *Prayer:*

*God, Please allow your forgiveness to seep into my soul, and cover up all my feelings of inadequacy. May I see me as you do. Help me to carry forward in freedom rather than sliding back into the comfortable pit. Like in the story, Jesus says in John 8:11, "I do not condemn you, either. Go. From now on sin no more." May the peace of your forgiveness take root and be the new solace for my spirit.*

# Day Fourteen: Shape Shifter

*1 Peter 2:9: But you are a chosen people, a royal priesthood, a holy nation, God's special possession, that you may declare the praises of him who called you out of darkness into his wonderful light (NIV).*

I am who I am because of the choices I've made in my past. From the day I stepped out of the clinic, my abortion largely molded and shaped my future. Sure, I have thought about going back and making a different choice. But it's not an option this side of heaven. I cannot go back in time as the person I am now and make a different choice. What I *can* do is live with the choice I made and move forward in healing and restoration. I *can* allow God's forgiveness to highlight those areas of my heart and heal the deep, dark places I've hidden.

Most days I am glad of who I have become in spite of my abortion. I am thankful that I can relate to other women who also have this scar. God has given me a gift in being able to watch their transformation as they see for the first time that they are not alone in their abortion. As they recognize that we are not so different from each other; we are the same. I watch as they come face to face with the harshness of the truth, but then I see God's light break through that darkness. I start to notice the slightest spark of hope in their eyes. And I see that hope grow as they start to accept forgiveness, feeling God's love wash over them. God has used my past to bring about some beautiful experiences in the present.

Still, there are days I wonder what life would have been like if I kept the baby. I know there is no use wondering about it, because I will never know. I only know what my life was like before and after the abortion.

I am in awe of a creator who continues to heal my heart and soul on the days when I wonder "what if." He doesn't give up, even though I sometimes do. He pursues me to the darkest places and shows me their beauty. He uses me, even when I think I'm useless. I do not want to live my life wondering what could have been, what might have been. I don't want my past to steal the joy of my future. Instead, I want to move forward, taking each step as God lights the path for me.

**Reflection Questions:**

- Is there anything that holds you back from believing God will restore you?

- What kind of "if onlys" are in your thoughts?

- Knowing you can't change the past, what is one thing you could do to change your future and move forward in God's grace?

_____

_____

_____

_____

_____

**Prayer:**

*Lord, my prayer is for restoration. Squash the "if onlys" and "what could have been" that roll in my mind like scenes from a movie. Help me to live my life in the present. I want to learn what I need to from the past, but move forward in your kingdom. Shape me and mold me in who you created me to be. Take my junk and make it into the crowning jewel of your kingdom. I know you can do this because you promise to use everything for your glory. You are the God of renewal, restore me inside and out.*

# Day Fifteen: The Great Exchange

*Isaiah 61:3: . . . to bestow on them a crown of beauty instead of ashes (NIV).*

Isaiah 61 has become one of my favorite Bible chapters. Reading these words, I can see God handing out replacement cards. "You were this. Now, in me, you are this." I need that reminder when I'm tempted to get bogged down in my failures.

We put so many expectations on ourselves and when we don't meet them, we begin to believe the lies that whisper to us. Here is what goes on in my mind during the waking hours. I want to read thirty-five books this year, study my bible daily and journal, write a novel, make encouraging cards for friends and family, practice the piano, bake goodies, make a good healthy dinner, exercise, keep the house clean, do laundry, *and* put it all away. Oh, and I work eight full hours too!

So I don't quite get to the exercise. And then I think about how fat I am and how unhealthy I'm becoming. And I don't quite get to making the cards I wanted or the journaling, so I feel like I have let all my friends down. I have a hard day at work and the thought of making dinner exhausts me, so I decide it will be better to eat out. So the voices begin to murmur that I'm a failure, and pretty soon I'm feeling worthless, guilty, and ashamed.

All these same feelings can be stirred by our abortion. But God replaces these lies with his truth from Isaiah 61:

- He gives us a crown of beauty for ashes (v. 3).
- He declares freedom for the captives (v. 1).
- He offers us a garment of praise rather than the spirit of despair (v. 3).
- He pours over us the oil of gladness instead of mourning (v. 3).

We are so busy *doing* rather than *being*. But these exchanges God promises are not a result of us *doing* anything. We just need to accept these free gifts. It's hard to just *be*, isn't it? But that is really all God wants from us.

When we understand this exchange God offers us, healing starts breaking through. This is where we begin to live as God created us. We shed the skin of our former self and become the women we were meant to be all along. Don't let that one moment in your past define who you are today. You are no longer that person. You are the Daughter of the risen King.

Don't believe in the lies anymore. It's time to replace them with God's truth.

**Reflection Questions:**

- What lies have you believed about yourself? About your abortion?

- What truth from Isaiah 61 or a different verse from the bible can you replace that lie with?

- What does God's Word say about you? In Ephesians 1:3-8, he says you are blessed. You are chosen. You are adopted. You are accepted. You are redeemed. You are forgiven. You are loved. Do you embrace these truths about yourself? Why or why not?

---

---

---

---

---

**Prayer:**

*Lord, please help me to exchange the lies with your truth and promises. Help me to believe that there isn't anything that I have to do for you. I simply need to believe. I know that I fall short at the end of the day, but I am not fair to myself to set higher expectations for than you ever intended me to meet. I no longer want to listen to the voices that say I am worthless, a failure, but let me cling to your Word and your voice that tells me I am worthy. I am yours.*

# Day Sixteen: Restoration

*Joel 2:25: I will restore to you the years that the swarming locust has eaten, the hopper, the destroyer, and the cutter, my great army, which I sent among you (ESV).*

The first time I read this verse, it choked me up. God said he would not only heal my heart, but he would also restore it. How could this be? I didn't believe restoration was possible, not only from my abortion, but from my life in general. I knew I was forgiven. But restored? I had screwed things up pretty badly. How could God bring any glory through that?

My parents and I didn't have the greatest relationship. We were broken in many ways. And when I reached seventeen, I decided I needed to get away. And so the downward spiral began. A lot of the choices I made during that time led me down the road to abortion. And it was hard to imagine that God could ever repair all the damage that resulted from that choice.

But our God is a God of miracles, and he has restored those broken places in so many ways to bring glory to his name. I have connected with many women who decided to abort, just like me; God is telling me that I am not alone. Through sharing my story, brick by brick, God is putting me back together.

To me, the process is like restoring an antique that was beautiful when it was first made. But through the years and many owners, it is now worn and damaged. Maybe a fire or flood has marked it up again. But you can still see its beauty, its potential. So you buy it, bring it home. Start learning the first steps toward bringing out its beauty again. And over time, you restore.

In the end, it looks a little different than the original, but better.

It's the same when God restores us. He takes our flaws and uses them to bring out the beauty in us. They fit in, like they were a part of the plan from the start. Each of us has our own story; there may be similarities, but it's our unique story that we can share. And we can use those stories of restoration to encourage others struggling in their own walk with God.

**Reflection Questions:**

- What would it look like if you believed in the promise that God wants to restore you?

- What does it look like for God to bring Glory to his name through your story?

- Is there one person, someone safe, that you can share your story and journey with?

_____

_____

_____

_____

_____

**Prayer:**

*Lord, you are faithful and merciful. I know your desire is to make me whole and healed, and restoration is part of that process. Your promises are true even if I don't believe they are for me. You continue to amaze me with your patience and love. You heal me just like you created me, knitting me back together. I am speechless seeing your mysterious ways. My past is not something that can I can change, but you have promised to restore the years the locusts have eaten, and I claim that promise. What was meant to harm me, you can turn around and make it work for good, for the saving of many. If I am blind, help me to see the beauty that you see in me, and the ways that you are restoring me day by day.*

# Day Seventeen: Redeemed

*Ephesians 1:7: In him we have redemption through his blood, the forgiveness of our trespasses, according to the riches of his grace (ESV).*

*Psalm 56:8: You keep track of all my sorrows. You have collected all my tears in your bottle. You have recorded each one in your book (NLT).*

Not only does God heal, forgive, and restore. He redeems.

I used to think that redemption meant the same thing as restoration. But when I studied the two words further, I found some differences. While restoration is a process, redemption is something God did once for all. By the cross he redeemed me, he bought me back, set me free. God exchanged my lies for truth, my sin for grace. He removed the scales from my eyes; so I could see that the door to the prison I built around myself had always been open.

It's almost enough to know the suffering he endured to rescue me, to bask in the love he showed for me by enduring the cross. But God goes a step further and says he keeps track of all my sorrows and has collected my tears in his bottle. Every one. Each wound. Each pain. Each heartbreak. Each tear shed. He has made note of these so I don't have to hold on to them. He wants to carry that burden for me so I can live in freedom.

Jesus' redemption shines every time I share my story and gives it a place in his kingdom. He uses my story to open the eyes of people unaware of the truths about abortion, whether they have experienced it or not. And because he carries my heartbreaks and burdens, I can live in freedom, inviting others to experience his redemption for themselves.

### Reflection Questions:

- Knowing God can use your story to help others, how does that make you feel?

- God wants to bear your burdens: Will you write them down, or speak them aloud to him?

_____

_____

_____

_____

_____

### Prayer:

*Father God, you have collected my tears in a bottle. I pray that you would show me the door to the prison I have built around myself, and help me to walk outside. Let your shining light warm and comfort me as I step onto unfamiliar ground. Open up my eyes to the truth and help me cling to the wonderful gift of grace that covers a multitude of sins. My abortion is no different from any of my other sins. I have been redeemed!*

# Day Eighteen: Forsake

*Psalm 27:10: Though my father and mother forsake me, the* LORD *will receive me (NIV).*

One day I came upon this verse, and I was not prepared for the host of vicious thoughts that came next. I thought about my child and what I gave up, what I forsook. Yes I found peace in knowing that God was able to receive her; but I threw her away. How could I have done that? What kind of person was I?

Moments like this are gut-wrenching. But God doesn't waste these moments. His truth may cut, but it cuts away the darkness so that only his light shines through. Years later, I came to learn the truth that Psalm 27:10 was not only meant to be applied to my child. It's also meant for me. The LORD will receive me too. He has loved me with an everlasting love I don't deserve. There is nothing I did to earn it, yet he loves me still.

God will never forsake us because of our past. He has unconditional love, compassion, and boundless grace. Overflowing grace that gives us hope and a future. I can't begin to understand how God does this; but he does. He gives grace for me, for you, and for the grumpy neighbor down the street.

Deuteronomy 33:27 says *"The eternal God is your refuge, and underneath are the everlasting arms."* No matter how low you feel today, how bad your life seems to be headed, how dark and painful the past, God's everlasting arms are under you. When you are tempted to give in to despair, forsake the lies with the truth and find refuge in God's never-ending love.

### Reflection Questions:

- Name a time in your life when your thoughts had you doubled over in guilt or shame?

- Take time to write down the truths that God says about you. (*Here are a few verses to get you started: Ephesians 1:3-8, Romans 8:1, Psalm 139*). Fight back the lies with the truth you discover.

_____

_____

_____

_____

_____

### Prayer:

*Lord, my prayer is that I would feel your everlasting arms underneath me, holding me up. I want to experience your grace and the true love that can only come from you. No matter my past, you love me, you will receive me. Oh let me be the lost one that you would leave the ninety-nine to find. I want to be found by you. I want to believe that I am worth searching for. I want to believe that you love me that much. I believe! Help me overcome my unbelief!*

# Day Nineteen: New Beginnings

*Isaiah 43:18-19: "Do not call to mind the former things, Or ponder things of the past. Behold, I will do something new, Now it will spring forth; Will you not be aware of it? I will even make a roadway in the wilderness, Rivers in the desert" (NASB).*

I've learned many lessons in this life. I have milestones imprinted on my soul; and I can still go back to that time and remember exactly what happened. April 27, 2013 marks one of these milestones. My husband had been having issues breathing and we brought him to the ER. Our visit resulted in ten days of hospitalization and open heart, quadruple-bypass surgery.

Through that one experience, I learned so many lessons:

- To take each step, moment by moment
- Not to sweat the super small stuff
- The sun will shine again
- To love like there is no tomorrow
- To let go of the past and live for today

After caring for my husband for months, I realized that I had been holding back for the first twelve years of our marriage. I had been keeping him at a distance. But the new, deeper love that blossomed between us during that next year left me speechless. Sometimes it takes those big milestone events to open our eyes so we can truly see.

It took almost losing my husband for me to finally see that I was worthy to be his wife.

Know this. Your past does not make you unworthy. It might have hurt you and broken you, but these things can be fixed. God can put you back together. When you are forgiven, *you are forgiven.* And it's not helpful to continue to "ponder the things of the past." So keep moving forward or you easily slide back into the muck. God has a new road for you to travel; will you be aware of it?

### Reflection Questions:

- What is in your past that keeps you stuck in the muck? What do you dwell on?

- If it seems impossible to move on, what is one small step forward you could take?

_____

_____

_____

_____

_____

### Prayer:

*Father God, I lay my burdens at your feet knowing it is only you that keeps me from backsliding into the pit. Please put your arms around me and give me the security that can only come from you. My one true Father. Your word tells me that my past no longer defines me. I am defined by who I am in Christ. When my thoughts of unworthiness begin to cascade into my heart, please gently nudge me and show me that I am worthy. You died so that I could live an abundant life.*

# Day Twenty: Sign Guy

*1 Corinthians 6:9-11: Or do you not know that the unrighteous will not inherit the kingdom of God? Do not be deceived; neither fornicators, nor idolaters, nor adulterers, nor effeminate, nor homosexuals, nor thieves, nor the covetous, nor drunkards, nor revilers, nor swindlers, will inherit the kingdom of God. Such were some of you; but you were washed, but you were sanctified, but you were justified in the name of the Lord Jesus Christ and in the Spirit of our God (NASB).*

There are signs all around us telling us what to do. Where to merge. What to buy. Where to go. People hold signs asking for money, protesting their causes, supporting their charity. One day, I was walking around our downtown area during a festival and came across a guy wearing a sandwich-board style sign. On it he had written every commandment and explained that if I had violated even one of these commands, I was condemned.

As I read through the sign, I realized I had broken every single commandment that was written on it.

Fortunately, I knew better. None of us are perfect, none of us make the cut. Maybe Sign Guy had good intentions; maybe he wanted to engage his audience and tell people that there's hope in Jesus' forgiveness. But he never got the chance. People buzzed around him, circling him and taunting him with angry words. Not a fruitful way to win people over to Christ.

I won't say nothing came from Sign Guy's efforts, because maybe it prompted someone to think more about their life and the path they were on. Maybe it turned someone around. But if I were Sign Guy and my purpose was to preach the good news, I would preach the Good News: There is hope in a Savior that died and rose again, to save us from ourselves, our sins, and our shortcomings. That's the message God wants us to hear—not in bold, condemning letters on a sign—but through the love and quiet blessings he pours upon us every day.

**Reflection Questions:**

- When you consider your abortion—which you might consider the worst of your sins—know this: The blood of Jesus covers it. What could you do today to live out of that love?

- Have you felt that "alone on an island" feeling—condemned, defeated. Read 1 Corinthians 6:9-11 aloud. Let the good news fall over you. "Such were some of you but now you have been . . ."

- What is one thing you can thank God for, a blessing he has given you? It doesn't matter how big or small. Sometimes it's a blessing just to get out of bed!

_____

_____

_____

_____

_____

**Prayer:**

*Lord, I see the signs all around me telling me what I should and shouldn't do. But you remain that constant, steady voice, always there, always listening. I know that you have always been there; I know without a doubt that you were always taking care of me. Please help me to see the signposts in my life; that they wouldn't be filled with empty condemnation, but with your love and compassion. That they would give me your hope and your peace that surpasses all understanding. You laid down your life to bring life to the full. I cannot begin to fathom the depth of love that required. Help me to feel this love you have for me.*

# Day Twenty-One: Grace

*Ephesians 2:8: For by grace you have been saved through faith; and that not of yourselves, it is the gift of God (NASB).*

Grace is a large, perfectly-wrapped present that God freely offers.

So the choice is ours. We can continue to wallow in our guilt, shame, and pain. Or we can let God have his way with us. Let him shine his light on our pain and accept his gift of forgiveness and healing.

It's easy to stop living after an abortion. Call it punishment; call it being paralyzed. But whatever you call it, it creeps up on you after something traumatic like an abortion. For many years I made the decision to live my life between the lines, not really embracing anything. If it weren't for God's grace, I would still be wallowing in my past.

We may tell God we are not ready; we are not good enough for him. We may put him off until a thousand tomorrows, thinking one of these days we will have it all together. But God opens up his hands and tells us it doesn't matter. He shows us grace right now. Infinite amounts of grace. Today. Grace for those moments when we want to kick ourselves. Grace for those times when we know we didn't quite get it right. Grace for the times we speak before we think. Grace for all the seasons in our life when we chose to lead rather than follow.

God offers new mercies every morning. Will you unwrap this beautiful gift?

### Reflection Questions:

- Where do you see yourself right now in God's eyes? Where would you like to be?

- Maybe you know all about grace, but what is one thing that stops you from accepting it?

- Maybe you have been living in freedom from your past. Take time to remember and thank God for all that he has done.

_____

_____

_____

_____

_____

### Prayer:

*Father God, I pray that if there is anything in me that needs your grace, you would bring it to my attention. Lord, you do not call us to be perfect, but to continue to walk in the ways of our perfect redeemer, Jesus. I don't want to wait until I am ready, because you have been waiting and ready for me since the beginning of time. Open up my heart and repair my past, help me move forward in victory.*

# Day Twenty-Two: Freedom

*Galatians 5:1: For freedom Christ has set us free; stand firm therefore, and do not submit again to a yoke of slavery (ESV).*

Whenever I think of freedom, I picture Mel Gibson in the final scenes of *Braveheart.* His dramatic dying words were shouting "Freedom!" to his fellow Scotsmen. I see that same tenacity in each woman who completes her study in our Surrendering the Secret group. She has been set free from prison. The chains have fallen off and she can now move forward with a purpose.

It is an honor to be a part of this process. To walk along side each participant and send them on their journey a little less broken than when they first walked through the door. They might not know it, but each group has been a part of my own healing process. Each group holds a special place in my heart. When I look at them, I see the face of God smiling back at me.

I serve a God that continues to work in me, healing me and making parts of me whole. He continues to open up new doors and invites me in for further restoration. God desires to do the same for you. So keep surrendering to God's will. Keep moving toward him. Take it from one who has already experienced his freedom: There's nothing like walking in the will of God to give you that peace that surpasses all understanding.

**Reflection Questions:**

• Write down any thoughts you have about what true freedom might feel like.

• If you haven't been a part of a Bible study group dealing with abortion, what holds you back?

• If you have been set free, in what ways do you live like it?

_____

_____

_____

_____

_____

**Prayer:**

*Lord, I pray for freedom that bursts forth from the top of my lungs! The kind of freedom that many have died for. The kind of freedom Jesus died for. You and you alone knows my needs, wants, hurts, and desires. You promised to grant me the desires of my heart. I desire you and wholeness and freedom from the shame. I want to move forward and align my life with your will. I want freedom to reign in my heart.*

# Day Twenty-Three: Comforter

*Psalm 119:76: O may Your lovingkindness comfort me, according to Your word to Your servant (NASB).*

After my abortion I remember coming home and sliding into bed under a brand-new comforter. It was oversized and the weight on top of me gave me a feeling of safety. During the years since, whenever I purchase a new comforter and slip under the covers that first night, the feelings of that day rush back.

Recently, I was sitting in church as the pastor talked about this idea of comfort. He pointed out that we can see a picture of God when mothers comfort others. ("As a mother comforts her child, so will I comfort you; and you will be comforted over Jerusalem." Isaiah 66:13, NIV). It struck me, quite obviously, that God wants to be *our* comforter.

So often, we try to use people and things to comfort us. We turn to our own earthly resources and hope they will make us feel secure. But only God has the ability to truly comfort. Only he can give us real safety. Everything else will let us down; the feelings of newness and security will fade, but God will not. As you draw near to him, he will continue to draw near to you, giving you his secure love and peace.

God promises to comfort us. The only question is: Will you draw near to him?

**Reflection Questions:**

- What is your "go to" for comfort?

- What were different ways you tried to comfort yourself after your abortion?

- What would it look like to allow God to be your comforter? In what ways could you find comfort in him?

_____

_____

_____

_____

_____

**Prayer:**

*Lord, there are so many ways I try to fill the emptiness, when what I need can only come from you. You and you alone should be my comfort, love, and safety. In you alone can I find this comfort. Help me to draw nearer to you and soak in your warm rays of light. Help me to trust in your promises, to not lean on my own understanding, but to allow your healing light to envelope me and hold me tight.*

# Day Twenty-Four: Hope

*Romans 15:13: May the God of hope fill you with all joy and peace in believing, so that by the power of the Holy Spirit you may abound in hope (ESV).*

In my city, we have a Garden of Hope. It's a beautiful memorial garden sheltered by tall bushes for privacy. The stone paths leading to and from the garden are lined with large rocks, each bearing a verse. A couple of memorial stones have been placed in the garden, where post-abortive women have the names of their children engraved. In the center of the garden stands a beautiful bronze statue; it depicts Jesus sitting next to a woman and holding her child in his arms. For those of us who have aborted our children, it is breathtaking, heartbreaking and restoring.

There was a time in my life when I had lost all hope. My future was bleak and darkness reigned. During this time, I felt that my boyfriend's abuse was something I deserved. I stayed with him, thinking there would be no one else who could love me or want me. I figured my life was as good as it was going to get.

Eventually, I dug myself out of this abusive relationship hole. But even after I thought I had put my past behind me, something still left me feeling burdened. I continued suffering in silence, unaware of how much my abortion secret still had a grip on my life, actions, and emotions. That is, until the Garden of Hope.

The Garden of Hope is just that. A garden of *hope*.

A place where we can mourn our children, but also a place that gives hope to mothers who have lost children to abortion. The garden shows us that we are not alone. That there are people out there who care enough about us to give us this place of hope. These people have the courage to stand up for women like you and me, and our children. They have given us a voice. And there in the center of their garden, we find the true source of hope for the future, a gentle Savior who holds us and our children in loving arms.

**Reflection Questions:**

- Is there something in your life that you have allowed as punishment, because you thought you deserved it?

- In what ways have you felt lost or powerless because of your abortion?

- Have you thought about joining an abortion healing group?

- If not, consider these other resources out there for you:
  https://gardenofhope.com
  http://surrenderingthesecret.com

_____

_____

_____

_____

_____

**Prayer:**

*Father, the feelings of dread and desperation can plague me from time to time. The choices I made in my life before and since my abortion have sent me down a road that I never realized I was going. Please show me the way to get back on my path, your will for my life. Help me make steps toward hope and healing. Guide my steps out of the dark tunnel and help me to see that my story is not finished being written. Every day you give us breath, there is hope. Lord, you are faithful and true. Help me to remember the promise of your Word: "Be strong and courageous. Do not fear or be in dread of them, for it is the* LORD *your God who goes with you. He will not leave you or forsake you" (Deut. 31:6* ESV*).*

# Day Twenty-Five: Saying Goodbye

*Isaiah 43:5-7: "Do not be afraid, for I am with you; I will bring your children from the east and gather you from the west. I will say to the north, 'Give them up!' and to the south, 'Do not hold them back.' Bring my sons from afar and my daughters from the ends of the earth— everyone who is called by my name, whom I created for my glory, whom I formed and made." (NIV).*

When I was in the abortion clinic, one of the rooms they led me to contained a machine; I discovered it was an ultrasound machine and learned this would be the first and only ultrasound of my baby. I remember wanting to ask if it was a boy or girl. Maybe having an answer to that question would have changed my mind; maybe seeing that picture would have made it more real to me than what I had been hearing. I don't know. But the screen was turned so I couldn't see. They didn't offer a look, and I didn't ask. I figured it was best I didn't know anyway.

Little did I know that many years later, in the early morning hours, a poem would come to me. I wrote furiously in the dark. I struggled with words like "child," "baby," "it," and "her." I kept writing "her," and when I went back to change it, I couldn't. There was a voice inside me, urging me, insisting *"It is a girl."* And about a year later, God would give me her name: Rebekah Hope.

There comes a point where we need to move on. We might find it helpful to name our children, pray about their gender or features. But eventually we must let them go. Saying goodbye is hard. But the peace we feel afterward is much better than the darkness we lived in. It gives us freedom to move past grief and press forward in grace, forgiveness, and truth.

As you continue your healing journey, remember that God has gathered all our lost ones close to himself. Ask him for the special strength to say good-bye and leave your child with him.

**Reflection Questions:**

- How do you say goodbye when you never said hello? How do you show your love when you took the life in the first place? Start by writing a letter to your child. What would you want to say to him/her that you never had the chance.

- If you let go, what do you believe God will restore back to you?

_____  _____

_____

_____

_____

_____

**Prayer:**

*Lord, help me say goodby to my child. I never met the life you had*

*created, I never knew them. But you knew them just as you knew me*

*when you created me. Help me move forward in freedom, release me*

*from the shackles of my past. Free me from the guilt and shame that is*

*so mixed up in me. I know what I did, and the reasons seemed so sound*

*at the time. I know I am not saying goodbye, but see you later. I pray*

*you would show me the ways that my life can be a living tribute to the*

*one(s) I lost and to give you the glory you deserve.*

# Day Twenty-Six: Rebekah Hope

*Romans 8:24-25: For in this hope we were saved. But hope that is seen is no hope at all. Who hopes for what they already have? But if we hope for what we do not yet have, we wait for it patiently (NIV).*

I saw you today. I was walking down the street. You turned around and waved at me with a little, cupped hand. Your ruby red lips covered in chocolate ice cream with a big, toothy grin. The sun reflected off your sheer blonde curls. But your eyes—your hazel brown eyes—are what captured my heart.

The day I first learned about you was no different than any other day. I knew it before they handed me the paper officially declaring your presence in my body. When it became official, I couldn't help but think of being a mom. I couldn't stop the hope from blossoming. But it wasn't long before my desires were crushed.

For weeks I fought for you. I blocked out their lies and cruel words. But in the end, I could not withstand the pressure, the force. I was weak. I was tired of the confrontations and the anger. I was weary of living in fear. I gave in and gave up. On you. And I'm sorry. I felt like I had no choice. But I was wrong; I made a choice. Looking back, I see I had all the power, yet I didn't know it. There are no excuses. I can only pray and hope for understanding. For forgiveness.

I do not need to look far for that hope. I feel it when God gives me glimpses of you, my child, here and there throughout my days. I see you in my poems, written in the middle of the night. I see you when I am facilitating groups of women who have also had abortions. I see you in song lyrics and in the music of my heart. I see you in the Gerber daisy I chose just for you.

Rebekah Hope, I know you are safe in the arms of Jesus. And I continue to trust and hope for what I haven't seen, knowing someday God will finally bring us together.

**Reflection Questions:**

- Have you thought much about your child, whether it was a boy or girl? What he or she would have looked like? If you feel led, journal your thoughts about your child.

- If you don't know, take some time to pray and seek God as to the sex of your child.

- Also take time to seek God for a name for your child. This can help you to grieve. (I want to stress that this is a process, so do not become discouraged if you do not immediately feel like God reveals anything to you about your child. This is something that could happen now, or it may come later. I do know that when you seek with your heart, God will provide the answers in his perfect timing.)

_____

_____

_____

_____

_____

**Prayer:**

*Lord, please let me not become disheartened in thinking of the child I lost, but let me rejoice in what you allow me to see, feel, and experience. I am excited for the day when I will meet my child(ren) face to face. I rejoice for you have forgiven me and you remember my sin no more! I know there are tough days ahead, but you are always with me through it all. I am your workmanship, whom you created. I am the apple of your eye. I rejoice for I once was dead, but now I am alive!*

# Day Twenty-Seven: Crossroads

*Romans 8:28-30: And we know that for those who love God all things work together for good, for those who are called according to his purpose. For those whom he foreknew he also predestined to be conformed to the image of his Son, in order that he might be the firstborn among many brothers. And those whom he predestined he also called, and those whom he called he also justified, and those whom he justified he also glorified (ESV).*

As I walked the road toward abortion, I was made to think I had no choice. In reality, I just didn't like my options. I couldn't see past the present into the future.

My choice came from a deep pit of fear within me; it told me I had no other way out. Once I had the abortion, relief cleared the darkness, for a time. But the truth eventually began to seep in. I did have a choice, but my eyes had been closed to other options. At the time I only saw two: failure or compliance. I couldn't see past the word "failure"—to the blessings it might have led to—so I chose compliance.

I let myself down, allowing others to bully me into a decision I didn't want and didn't believe in. I chose to abort out of a desire to keep the peace and to put everything behind me. It was just the way it had to be. Sure, I faced huge pressure from others, but I take responsibility for my ultimate choice, because in the end, it was up to me to take the harder road.

We've all been at the crossroads, facing a huge decision we didn't want to make. And we've all made choices we regret. But regardless of the choices we have made, God can still use us. If we are honest about our past and hand it over to him, we can reach a new crossroads: where God will take everything and make it work together for good. All of our ingredients by themselves might seem awful. But when you mix them all together, God can whip up something truly wonderful, mistakes and all.

**Reflection Questions:**

- What brought you to your abortion decision?

- How can God use all your mistakes and work it for his good?

- What steps can you take to let God use you and your story to help others who also might find themselves at a similar crossroads in their lives?

_____

_____

_____

_____

_____

**Prayer:**

*Lord, I know you have promised in your word that you work all*

*things together for good. Please help me to claim the promises of your*

*word. I pray that you would take my abortion and use it to your*

*advantage. Make something beautiful out of the darkest, ugliest parts*

*of me. Grant me the strength I need to share my story with those who*

*you put in my path. Please grant me your peace and open my eyes to*

*the fields of beauty around me that you have created. I am so grateful*

*that you would do this for me! You do work all things for your good!*

# Day Twenty-Eight: Transformation

*Romans 12:2: Do not be conformed to this world, but be transformed by the renewal of your mind, that by testing you may discern what is the will of God, what is good and acceptable and perfect (ESV).*

I love watching butterflies. They are delicate and soar high above, floating on the gentle summer breeze. But they weren't always butterflies. At one time they were caterpillars, some brilliantly colored, some grotesque, and some downright scary. They crawled around on their bellies inch by inch, until one day they were wrapped up in a cocoon and transformed.

God did that for me at one time. He wrapped me tightly in his cocoon and told me that it would be okay. He promised me that he would take care of everything, that he would remember my sin no more.

I once was walking dead, but God transformed me, my life. He took me and lifted me up. In the safety of his arms, he cut away the shame and guilt that ruled my life and replaced it with worthiness, love, and hope. And now I can soar in freedom from the past.

Transformation. Freedom.

These words float with the beauty of a butterfly. But they are born through the struggle of an ugly caterpillar. Truth is, we don't have to make ourselves perfect before we can come to God. He finds us worthy of his love even when we are crawling in the darkness as ugly caterpillars. He made a difference in my life by telling and showing me I mattered. And if I was worthy of his transformation, then I know without a doubt that you are too.

**Reflection Questions:**

- Do you feel like a butterfly or a caterpillar? Why?

- If you feel like a caterpillar, ask God to wrap you in his cocoon and transform you into that beautiful butterfly you are meant to be.

- If you feel like a butterfly, ask God to work in you so that you can truly soar and be free.

- If you feel like neither of these, take time to journal those thoughts.

_____

_____

_____

_____

_____

**Prayer:**

*Lord, you love with an everlasting love that defies all logic and understanding. Let me see this love that you have for me. Let me feel that it is for me and not someone else. I want to see my worth through your eyes rather than my own skewed vision. I am not doing well transforming on my own, please take me and mold and shape me, transform me into who you created me to be.*

# Day Twenty-Nine: Ripples

*Matthew 25:40: "The King will reply, 'Truly I tell you, Whatever you did for one of the least of these bothers and sister of mine, you did for me.'"*(NIV).

We all want to be her—that superwoman we see in the grocery store. Flawless hair and makeup, dressed to the nines. She looks like she's got everything perfectly put together. Here's what we don't understand; she doesn't really exist!

Underneath the outer layers, we are all broken vessels. It is what God does with these broken places that is miraculous. When God puts us back together, we have a little more character than before. Our flaws become special, even beautiful. We can relate more easily to one another. We don't have to act like we have it all together, because we discover that we have similar fears, shortcomings, and feelings of inadequacy. While the masks we wear might fool others, we can't fool ourselves. And it's a relief when we finally stop pretending we are perfect and instead start leaning on God's grace.

Sometimes, when I think about my abortion, I question how I could have done something like that. But then I remember I have been forgiven, and I remind myself to ask, "What can I do from here?" or "How do I make it right?" The short answer, of course, is that we can't *do* anything to make up for it. But by sharing our stories, we *can* help others see. Maybe we can prevent others from having an abortion; or more importantly, maybe we can relate to another woman who is struggling with her abortion. We can show her there is hope and she doesn't need to suffer in silence. That she doesn't need to pretend— with us or with God.

I once heard a sermon where the pastor compared our lives to ripples in a pond. I don't remember the exact words, but the concept stuck with me. We make our own ripples and affect other people, just as their ripples have affected us.

What we do with our lives, our choices, they matter. Though we cannot change our past, we can make new choices today, sending out positive ripples in the lives of those around us.

**Reflection Questions:**

- Think back to a time when someone affected your life in a positive way. What was the ripple affect that it created in your own life?

- What kind of ripples are you creating?

_____

_____

_____

_____

_____

**Prayer:**

_Lord, help me to see past my brokenness, and to believe that you have made me beautiful inside and out. Help me to see the hope I have in you. I pray my ripples positively flow outward and affect those around me. Help me to realize my value and the worth that you see in me. Don't let me get caught up in the compare and despair, but live the life that you have laid out for me. You have redeemed me, I am yours!_

# Day Thirty: Identity

*2 Corinthians 5:17: Therefore if anyone is in Christ, he is a new creature; the old things passed away; behold, new things have come (NASB).*

I was once afraid. My secret held tight in the depths of my soul, and I felt defined by it. Everything I did or didn't do seemed to wrap around that one choice I made when I was eighteen.

But then I found freedom. Freedom in healing. Freedom in the shadow of God's wings, where he promises to shelter me. Freedom in sharing this secret.

I remember sitting in a meeting one day discussing revisions to the Surrendering the Secret Bible study I help facilitate. At one point during the meeting I spoke these words, "When I was post-abortive . . ." Once the words exited my mouth I actually thought about them, and I started laughing. What had I just said? "When I *was* post-abortive." I laughed with joy because I realized that being "post-abortive" was in my past. That my choice to abort no longer defined who I am.

That moment has stuck with me. It's not that I went back in time and didn't have the abortion. The choice was still there, the consequences. But God had healed my heart, and he used my experience for his glory. He took the bad and used it for good. And I knew he was doing a work in me; I had seen it in all the groups I led. But to heal me so completely, as if it hadn't happened—or at the very

...e a distant memory—that was beyond anything I ever

...erve an amazing God.

...ontinue to seek the light. Because in the light I don't have to

...or pretend. In the light I am free to live. In the light God's grace is

...al and far reaching. In the light I will continue to stomp out fear.

Post-abortive is no longer my identity. I am reaching out to better things.

**Reflection Questions:**

- How tightly do you hold on to your secret?

- In what ways has your identity been shaped by your abortion?

- God can make beauty from your ashes—he can use your abortion for good. Read through Isaiah 61 and journal your thoughts.

_____

_____

_____

_____

_____

**Prayer:**

*Lord, you know my heart. You know my fears, hopes, and dreams. Please shine your healing light on the places that need to be brought out of darkness. I know that it might sting at first, but I trust in you God, because you are forever faithful. The depths you go to heal me are astounding. I cannot even begin to fathom the extent you will go to restore me. I pray that one day I will be able to stand up and shout, "I* am beauty from ashes in the flesh!"

# Day Thirty-One: Next Step

*Proverbs 3:6: In all your ways submit to him, and he will make your paths straight (NIV).*

It's easy to get caught up in all this newfound truth and purpose. To ask what you should be doing now that you've started working toward freedom and healing. As you come to the end of this devotional journey, you might be wondering what comes next. Here's what I have learned: We are all individuals, and we each have our own path to follow.

My story started with a poem about my child. My journey continued with an abortion Bible study, sidewalk counseling, and eventually facilitating Bible studies myself for women in my town. Recently, it's led to a blog and this devotional. It continues to be a process. I feel like I am always asking, "Okay God, what next? How will you use my story next?"

One important word of caution I would offer is to be careful *who* you share your story with. Be wary of people that might want to twist your words and use it against you. Watch out for those who just want to debate. If you are ready to start sharing your story, God will lead you to the right people. Ask for his wisdom and he will give you discernment.

So what is *your* next step? What is God speaking to you? Is it to seek out a healing group? Maybe join a Bible study to learn more about God? Tell your husband what you did when you were young? Whatever it is, I know God is speaking it to you now; maybe there is small nagging feeling in your soul. So take a few moments today and write about those thoughts here. Where do you sense God asking you to move? Then write some action steps: What will it take for you to move forward? Maybe you don't know yet, and that's okay too. Meditate on it, let it simmer.

If you continue to trust him with your journey, God will make your path straight.

_____

_____

_____

_____

_____

**Prayer:**

*Lord, I am confidant you have a purpose for me. My prayer is that you would help me to see what my next step is. Light my path so it is clear. Give me the gift of discernment for what and whom I should share my story. Protect me with your shield of faith if someone tries to come against me. As I close the pages of this book, help me to begin my journey toward the freedom you have promised me.*

*The LORD bless you, and keep you;*
*The LORD make His face shine on you,*
*And be gracious to you;*
*The LORD lift up His countenance on you,*
*And give you peace.*
*(Numbers 6:24-26 NKJV)*

# Acknowledgements

Thank you to my husband. No matter what crazy idea I have you always support me and tell me to go for it. Always.

Thank you to my sister and best friend. You are my personal cheerleader and your belief in me gives me strength. It would be nice if I could borrow the elves once in a while.

Thank you to my friends who write and those who do not. You have all had a place in my world. You have encouraged me, believed in my writing and pushed me to finish and given me courage to put my heart out there.

Thank you to my Garden of Hope friends. Mary, Julie, Denise. You have truly changed the direction of my journey. You have shown me grace in multiple ways and I can't imagine my life without your friendship, love and support.

# About the Author

M. L. Alvarez lives in West Michigan with her husband Rick and red lab Blaze.  When not writing, she enjoys drawing and watercolor painting.

[1]. Mark Hall "Your Own Jesus" page 51

Made in the USA
Monee, IL
07 February 2020

21467107R10068